JOURNEY TO inner balance

90-DAY **GUIDED JOURNAL**

that empowers you towards consistency, balance and reaching your true potential using

MSBR

CHAIM LEVY

REVIEWS ARE CRUCIAL FOR EVERY AUTHOR!

Would you consider taking two minutes of your time and leaving an honest review on Amazon? Just search my title, click on the book listing and scroll down until you see **"Write a Review for this Product"**

Volume 1

Journey to Inner Balance:
A guided journal that empowers you toward consistency and life in harmony using MSRB techniques.

Edited, Typesetting & Cover Design by:
Lyndsay Stanley, Stonecreek Editing Services

Paperback ISBN:	978-1-998319-10-7
Hardcover ISBN:	978-1-998319-12-1
Premium Ed. Hardcover ISBN:	978-1-998319-11-4

For discounts on bulk orders or for general inquiries, please visit www.MSBRjournal.com or email: hi@msbrjournal.com

DISCLAIMER:

The author has made every attempt to provide information that is accurate and complete, but this book is not intended as a substitute for professional medical advice. This book is not meant to be used, nor should it be used, to diagnose or treat any medical or psychological condition. Readers are advised to consult their own medical advisors whose responsibility it is to determine the condition of, and best treatment for, the reader.

Table of Contents

Forward 1

PART 1 Preparing For a Long Journey

Chapter 1: Beginning Your Journey Towards Harmony 8
What is MSBR anyway?

Chapter 2: To Get There You Have to Learn Balance 16
Balancing your Mind, Soul, Body and Relationships

Chapter 3: Getting on the Right Path 19
Using Journaling as a way to benefit from MSBR

Chapter 4: Navigating with Positivity 24
What MSBR looks like in real life.

Chapter 5 Journey to Greatness: Setting Goals & Achieving Them 26
How to set goals that won't burden you.

The Spiraling Sketchbook 40

PART 2 Embarking on the Trail of Life

How to Use this Journal 43

The 90-Day MSBR Journal 46

This journal belongs to:

....

I'm starting to explore on: (date)

What message would you send to your future self in 90 days?

....

....

To the remarkable students who have walked through the doors of my classroom over the last two decades.

Your enduring support, thirst for greatness, and enthusiasm have enriched my life with tried knowledge and the inspiration to create this guided journal.

To my wife.
This book is a snapshot of the amazing life and home we've built together- a journey filled with exploration and balance. Thank you for believing in me from day one.

And to God for the opportunity to share.

CHECK OUT THE BONUS MATERIAL

The MSBR Trail is rewarding, but it can be a challenging uphill climb. So, I've developed some additional resources for your journey, including writing prompts for when you get stuck on those blank journaling pages, self-reflection questions that will push you to go deeper, motivational messages recorded by the author, for those slow days, goal-setting inspiration, and thought-provoking bonus content that will act like binoculars, making MSBR concepts even more clear to you. And so much more!

SCAN THE QR CODE OR VISIT:

www.msbrjournal.com/msbr-resources-library

Forward

Welcome to a new way of doing life.

Your emotional and mental health is something that you'll need to guard and nurture all your life. There will be seasons when you feel like you've got it figured out and don't really need any help. And then the storm will come out of nowhere. The flood waters will climb and surround you. And you will go down because you weren't wearing your life jacket.

MSBR can be your life jacket. It allows you to keep your head above water as you navigate the waves.

You've picked up this journal for one of three reasons:

- Intrigued by the cover
- You love writing and or journaling.
- You want to try something new to get your thoughts out

All are pretty good reasons. While I did want this journal to be 'fun,' entertainment value wasn't my whole intention. This journal is a little different than others you might come across at a department store in that it uses, as its foundation, a unique theory of self-growth that I developed and have been using for over a decade called MSBR. Building your life around the MSBR model is like ensuring your compass is pointed north and keeping it ready in your hand for all of life's journeys.

M Mind

S Soul

B Body

R Relationships

What is MSBR?

For over two decades, I have been teaching university-age students. Over the years, I've been blessed with amazing students and opportunities to have a positive impact on their lives. And from where I stand, that is mostly down to the fact that I teach what I've personally learned in my life.

For instance, my journey towards self-esteem and self-worth led me to create a course dedicated to these crucial aspects. Similarly, as I grappled with the complexities of stepping into the business world while seeking balance, I designed a course addressing this challenge. Integrating religion harmoniously into life was another puzzle I worked on for years, which subsequently became a course. This pattern continued, each course evolving and refining through collaboration with my students—my platform for idea evolution.

MIND

Knowledge sets the floor,
imagination builds the roof.

SOUL

Consistent actions nourish the
soul's transformation.

BODY

Our bodies are the vessels that carry
us toward elevation.

RELATIONSHIPS

Like the notes in a beautiful symphony,
our relationships with others must be
in harmony for us to become the best
version of ourselves.

We find this concept in the Talmud, attributed to Akiva ben Joseph, attributed to having thousands of students. He states that as a teacher, he has learned more from his students than from anything else.

My ultimate aspiration is to impart knowledge that equips my students for the long game. I firmly believe that this wisdom lays the foundation for a stable home and life. To my dismay, I wasn't exactly seeing this in my students. So, I started to dig deeply into what might be going on.

The students that I teach are primarily comprised of university-aged students who are taking one or two years to study abroad. Anyone who has ever lived far from home knows how difficult it can be to suddenly find yourself in another culture without your friends or family around. While still ex-pats, they thrived while enrolled in my courses, but when it came time to go home, the growth they had achieved seemed to slip away, leaving them disheartened.

Witnessing this struggle sparked a strong conviction within me: I needed to find a balanced system for helping these kids take care of themselves holistically so that they would no longer be discouraged and lost. Years of analysis were dedicated to understanding their struggles and devising practical solutions. Thus, the MSBR system was conceived—a haven, a guiding light of rejuvenation, crafted to reignite the flame within my students during moments of low spirits and inspire them to re-engage with their aspirations. Over the years, I've incorporated MSBR into many of my courses for university students and realized that a companion tool for MSBR is a guided journal. And Voila! We have "Journey to Inner Balance: A Guided Journal: A guide that empowers you towards consistency and life in harmony using MSBR."

Okay so I've answered how MSBR came to be. but why should you care about MSBR at all?

If you've picked up this journal, chances are you are searching for meaning, peace, and inner balance in your life. Maybe these concepts have been elusive up to this point in your life. Well, adapting the principles of MSBR to your life, using this journal, can really help you restructure your life and give you that inner balance that you have been looking for. It's simple, really.

We all want peace.
We all want balance.
We all want tools for success.

And MSBR can help you achieve those things.

By living out the MSBR model slowly but surely, you'll start to experience more peace, more balance, and [as a result] more success in life. But you have to do the work of honest introspection, detailed self-expression, and intentional planning. There will be days when you don't want to do this. And that's why I've developed a secondary tool to help you.

My website is chock-full of resources that will help you answer some hard questions, give you some inspiration when setting up your goals, writing prompts when you're stuck on those journaling pages, and have thought-provoking reflection questions that will push you to dive deeper.

And there's one more thing...

Ill be going on this journey with you

For each of the 12 weeks, I've provided a title page with a QR code to the recordings library on my website. Please be sure to tune into these recordings, as they'll give you even more insights along your MSBR journey and additional practical tips for adapting the concepts into your everyday life. All you have to do is scan the QR Code, and you're off to the races!

So, if youre ready, its time to tie up your boots and start studying your map. Lets go!

part 1
PREPARING FOR A LONG JOURNEY

chapter 1

Beginning Your Journey Towards Harmony: What is MSBR Anyway?

When Dr. Martin Seligman became the incoming president of the American Psychological Association, he pushed for a change. Rather than focusing only on mental illness, he stressed the importance of looking at the positive aspects of life's foundations. This shift marked the beginning of positive psychology interventions aimed at improving different parts of life and fostering overall well-being. It emphasized the significance of finding balance across life's essentials (Rusk & Waters, 2015).

Dr. Seligman highlighted the importance of specific core elements in life pillars as crucial factors of life. These components play a pivotal role in not just bringing happiness and joy but also in contributing to personal fulfillment, emphasizing that finding balance across life's pillars makes life meaningful and significant. Using his direction, I have garnered inspiration for Seeking Knowledge – Taking Action- Self-Care- and Relationships – with MSBR.

The mystical teachings in Judaism talk much about living a balanced life. The traditions of Etz Haim say that opposite forces of judgment and mercy can work together to create balance. These teachings focus on harmony between seemingly opposing spiritual energies.

Our journey is similar as we try to find harmony between different pillars of our life, each tugging at its own direction. It is from these foundations that MSBR emerged. Here's another way to think about it: MSBR is like the quarterback in a football game, leading the team and setting them up for a collective WIN! No teammate is left behind. The quarterback [MSBR] ensures the touchdown occurs for everybody. MSBR ignites a winning momentum, propelling every significant aspect of your life forward and allowing you to live a victorious and balanced life.

So, lets go deeper into what we mean by Mind, Soul, Body, and Relationships.

MIND

The "M" in MSBR stands for the MIND—a symbol of perpetually adopting a lifestyle driven by constant learning. It's about navigating life's chaos and striving to find order and meaning within it. Our mind embarks on a ceaseless journey, seeking fresh avenues to love, explore, decide, and comprehend. Recognizing that our potential is tied to the expansiveness and strength of our mind, we understand that limitations on the mind inevitably constrain us as well.

The more we know, the more we grow. The stronger our mindset, the stronger we are. So, the idea here is to set up a lifestyle where we are always learning new things and improving our mindset. Our mind is exploring new ways to love, be productive, find fulfillment, make decisions, find solutions to problems, and embark on emotional stability. If it is limited, so are we. Our mind is a muscle. The "M" of MSBR helps us strengthen it.

In "Mind," we set two types of goals: 1) Goals that will broaden our strength to explore ourselves and our next steps. 2) Goals that help us to approach life in a healthy, positive, and productive way. We gather vital knowledge by reading more books, listening to more podcasts and lectures, meditating, and working toward self-awareness.

A strong mind is not one that never fails but one that perseveres in the face of adversity. constantly learning and growing.

SOUL

The "S" in MSBR stands for SOUL. The soul is on an upward journey, consistently pushing the boundaries toward greatness. Actions are directly tied to the soul's journey and its accumulation of wisdom. The soul's actions, both positive and negative, determine its path and experiences in this life and potentially in future lives. In this pillar, we set goals that will affect our inner soul, the real me.

Small positive actions may seem inconsequential on their own, but when consistently practiced, they can accumulate and lead to profound transformations. Just as individual drops of rain collectively form a powerful river, these small acts of kindness, perseverance, and compassion pave the way for significant and beautiful changes in our lives and the world around us. They serve as the building blocks of a brighter, more harmonious future, reminding us that even the smallest deeds can create a ripple effect of positivity and inspire others to join in creating a better world.

In "SOUL," we set meaningful and achievable goals that lead our inner self toward greatness.

The beauty of positive actions is that they not only brighten the world but also illuminate your soul"

-unknown

BODY

The "B" in MSBR stands for Body. One can buy the most aromatic fragrance, but if it is cased in a box that is spoiled, it will be tarnished. The soul and mind are encased in our bodies. We need to take care of the vessel that holds our greatness. "Body" is about setting time aside to take care of the vessel that GOD has given us.

Taking care of our bodies is an essential investment in our overall well-being. When we prioritize our physical health through exercise, nourishing food, self-care, and "me time," we experience increased energy and vitality and a positive impact on our mental and emotional state.

A healthy body forms the foundation for a robust and resilient mind, allowing us to better manage stress, stay focused, and find the motivation to pursue our goals. It's a holistic approach to self-improvement, where the well-being of our body translates into a more balanced and fulfilling life, enabling us to thrive in all aspects of our journey.

Setting goals within the "body" pillar aims to cultivate vitality, energy, and inner peace.

"A strong healthy body is the best safeguard against the storms of life"

– Thomas Jefferson

RELATIONSHIPS

The "R" in MSBR stands for Relationships. In the intricate tapestry of our lives, we seamlessly transition between multiple roles at once, each demanding unique facets of our personality and emotions. We are devoted partners, cherished friends, loving grandchildren, dependable siblings, diligent employees, curious students, and a caring aunt or uncle. While these relationships paint a rich tapestry of our identity, they also shape how the world perceives us.

However, it's crucial to recognize that these relationships are not isolated islands but interconnected threads in the fabric of our existence. When one of these relationships faces turmoil or significant conflict, it has a profound ripple effect, casting shadows over our overall well-being.

WHAT RELATIONSHIPS DO I HAVE?

In the intricate dance of existence, we find ourselves adorned with a mosaic of roles, each adding depth and dimension to the tapestry of our lives. As individuals, we navigate a vast array of relationships and responsibilities, embodying the essence of a son, father, grandfather, uncle, teacher, boss, coach, and best friend, among many others. These roles, ever-shifting and intertwining, define our identities and shape our interactions with the world around us. They reflect the multifaceted nature of human existence, offering glimpses into the myriad facets of our being. Join me on a journey through the labyrinth of roles we inhabit, each adding its own hue to the canvas of our existence.

Using the lines on the next page, list the different roles you play in life. We will be referring back to this in your relationship goals throughout the next twelve weeks of journaling and adding even more as we go.

The emotional and psychological strain that arises from a troubled relationship or major conflict within it touches us deeply, making it challenging to navigate other aspects of our lives with the same effectiveness, productivity, and stability.

The weight of turmoil in one of our relationships can bear heavily on our shoulders, influencing our emotional and mental states. This can create a sense of imbalance, pulling us in various directions and hindering our ability to concentrate and perform at our best. Maintaining a healthy balance in our multifaceted lives becomes a formidable task when one of the critical relationships that contribute to our self-perception is shaken. To preserve our well-being and holistic equilibrium, it becomes essential to address conflicts and disruptions in these key relationships, recognizing that the health of our interwoven identities and relationships is intrinsic to our overall sense of fulfillment and harmony.

"In the grand orchestra of life, each relationship, (and) each role we play, adds a unique note, and when played together, they create a beautiful symphony of harmony."

- Unknown

THEY'RE ALL INTERCONNECTED

When one element is significantly out of sync, it impacts us on a holistic level. This guided journal aims to align and empower your life's four pillars—Mind, Soul, Body, and Relationships. By fostering understanding and offering a simple-to-use platform for improvement, it guides you toward achieving your greatest goals in life.

Understanding MSBR

The beauty of MSBR is that it can be used to analyze almost any aspect of life and answer the 'big questions' of life and meaning. For example, let's dig into this meaty question:

Why is it challenging to love others if we don't love ourselves first?

The answer lies in the way we perceive the world and navigate life—it's shaped by our mental state. How we see the world is influenced by our inner experiences. If you don't love yourself, then it's hard to see the world as a loving place. If we are frustrated or angry, it can diminish our patience, altering how we interact with the world, even if the matter is totally unrelated to the cause of our anger. If a vital aspect of life is out of balance, it affects the entire "system." A heated argument with a family member can disrupt our focus on work, just as dissatisfaction with our self-image can impede motivation to work or explore opportunities. The solution lies in simplifying life's fundamentals and progressing in harmony across all domains simultaneously.

What MSBR Is & Isn't

Self-help is a huge industry. It's never been easier to find blog articles, social media memes, and entire books that will make guarantees like 'a new and better you NOW!' The truth is that while these items might help some people, they will do the opposite for most. That's because human beings are complex and unique. These quick-fix models are akin to attempting to fix a leaky pipe with duct tape. The problem hasn't been solved. It might work for a while, but the underlying problem will take more know-how, time, and effort to fix.

Before you get really deep into the MSBR technique, I want to lay out for you exactly what to expect from MSBR and yourself. You'll have to know what MSBR is and what it isn't.

MSBR Isn't...

- A quick fix
- A box to check off on your to-do list
- An "easy" read
- A social media trend

MSBR Is...

- A holistic way of life. A recipe to discover new things about yourself and others.
- A path for self-accountability and necessitates commitment
- A wave of stability and positivity in your life

chapter 2

To Get There You Have to Learn Balance:

Balancing your Mind, Soul, Body and Relationships

In the current fast-paced and interconnected world, finding balance is a pressing need for our generation. The digital age suffocates us with an avalanche of information, constant notifications, and digital distractions that demand our attention. Amidst this chaos, creating a balance becomes crucial to manage our time and mental energy effectively. Social media makes it easy for us to compare ourselves with everyone else. It is like a gallery of idealized portraits that are not realistic. But still, they make us all feel inadequate. If we have balance in our lives, we can easily see an unrealistic image of someone else and know that that is not reality. And we don't think another thought of it.

Another aspect of our culture that stops us from easily finding balance is the immensity of opportunities that are available to anyone now. And most of those opportunities are annoyingly portrayed as being easy! If you're going to successfully navigate through all the nonsense without losing your mind, you need to set priorities and boundaries for your time and focus.

The world is a noisy place with endless options. Finding balance and tuning out every once in a while is just one key to keeping your sanity and well-being.

Balance, our guiding compass on our ongoing journey of self-improvement, involves harmonizing mind, soul, body, and relationships. Picture this journey as a tightrope walk, demanding equilibrium to move forward without stumbling. Just as a tightrope walker carefully distributes weight and attention, we, too, must balance our mental, spiritual, and physical well-being while managing diverse relationships in life. Wisely allocating our resources—time, effort, and attention—across careers, relationships, health, personal growth, and spiritual pursuits is crucial. Imbalance risks burnout, strained relationships, and a diminished sense of well-being.

An aggressive imbalance in one foundational part of life often has a ripple effect, negatively impacting other areas. Striking a balance and pursuing harmony between different aspects of life is generally more sustainable and conducive to well-rounded personal development and long-term happiness.

Attaining equilibrium or stability demands mindfulness, conscious decisions, and the courage to change things up when needed. It's a purposeful voyage through life's twists and turns, where balance consistently guides us in the right direction towards continuous growth and betterment of our mind, soul, body, and the relationships we embrace.

And journaling is a major tool for achieving this balance. I've set up this journal in particular to serve as the companion on our journey, offering a "bird's eye view" of life and a strategic roadmap for progress.

Why does this generation need balance more than others?

This generation battles a relentless onslaught of stressors. From unforgiving academic demands to the fierce competition in the job market, the unending pursuit of financial stability to match the previous generation, and the constant grip of the 24/7 digital world — we're caught in a whirlwind. These pressures mercilessly fuel challenges, leaving us with no choice but to fight back, seeking the desperate support we need.

Then, there's the realm of social media—a breeding ground for self-doubt, anxiety, and depression. We're incessantly bombarded with carefully curated portrayals of others' seemingly flawless lives. It's a battleground where comparisons run rampant, pushing us to the edge and forcing us to seek tools to salvage our sanity from the clutches of this digital beast.

As if that weren't enough, the very fabric of our social connections has frayed, with shifting family dynamics, vanishing community bonds, and an unrelenting drive for mobility in modern life. These changes viciously claw at our mental and emotional well-being. We need to even the playing field!

chapter 3

Getting on the Right Path:

Using Journaling as a Way to Benefit from MSBR

So, we've talked a lot about MSBR, a self-growth holistic mindset that promotes balance.

But how do you get there?

One of the most useful tools for making MSBR become part of your everyday life is journaling.

Your journal is a safe friend who will never tell your secrets. You can express anything you want without any judgment. Each new page is an opportunity for encouragement, self-discovery, and comfort through difficult times.

1. EXPRESS.
2. SET-GOALS.
3. TAKE ACTION.
4. REPEAT.

A journal is a friend that listens without judging, comforts without speaking, and takes even your wildest dreams seriously.

Having a regular journaling practice can make all of the planning and intention needed for MSBR into something you barely even think about. Use your journal to:

- **Make plans to nourish your mind, soul, body, and relationships.**
- **Set specific goals using the SMART model (see the next section for detailed instructions).**
- **Expand your mind by asking difficult questions and finding the answers about yourself and the world around you.**
- **Track the various areas of your life and ask yourself, 'Am I balanced?'**

Once you know that, self-realization clicks on like a switch, and you'll be free to pursue your hopes and dreams and no longer be weighed down by your limiting beliefs, self-doubt, lack of awareness, etc.

If you're not already a journaler, it can be hard to start up a routine of journaling. I know that when I started to journal, I'd flip open a blank page, and to my dismay, the previous page was dated three months earlier! *Three months without journaling!*

It's always good to get your thoughts and emotions out in a private context but to really get at the rich benefits of journaling; you'll want to be intentional and develop a daily routine. How?

HERE ARE SOME TIPS:

- Write in your journal at the same time every day/ or time of the week. What is the best time of day for you to get your thoughts out? When do you think the clearest? If youre a morning person, you might want to set aside a couple of minutes in the morning to journal. If you like to stay up at night, you might want to schedule it then,before bed.

- Try to journal in the same place each time. This way, your brain and your muscles will remember that this is where you write, and over time, youll find that the words just flow out of you. Do you have a train ride home from work or school? This is a great place to journal!

- Start small. Plan to write just a few lines to start out

- Dont Overthink. Journaling is supposed to be relaxing, so dont overthink what you should write. Dont even worry about your grammar and spelling. Just write. Think about flow, not accuracy.

"Journaling is like whispering to one's self and listening at the same time."

-Mina Murray from
Bram Stoker's "Dracula"

BENEFITS
OF JOURNALING

GAIN CLARITY & ORGANIZATION

Helps in organizing thoughts, plans, and goals and creating a clearer understanding of what needs to be done.

EMOTIONAL RELEASE

Serves as an emotional outlet, allowing you to express feelings and thoughts that might be difficult to share verbally.

ALLEVIATES STRESS

Writing can be a form of stress relief, helping to alleviate feelings of anxiety and tension by putting thoughts on paper.

GOOD FOR CONFLICT RESOLUTION

Writing about challenges and issues often leads to new perspectives and potential solutions.

GROW IN POSITIVITY

Writing out your thoughts and feelings can generate a positive wave in your life that uplifts you in both challenging and joyful moments.

BENEFITS OF JOURNALING

ENHANCES SELF-AWARENESS

Reflecting on your thoughts and actions increases self-awareness and a better understanding of your personal patterns, values, and strengths, leading to a better understanding of who you are.

BOOSTS YOUR CREATIVITY

Stimulates creativity and innovative thinking by providing a space for free expression and exploration of ideas.

IMPROVES YOUR COMMUNICATION ABILITIES

Enhances communication skills as it encourages the articulation of thoughts and feelings.

chapter 4

Navigating with Positivity:

What MSBR Looks Like in Real Life

Lost amidst the vast expanse of the shimmering sea, Morris embarked on a surfing expedition, armed with a zeal to conquer the majestic waves. Each crest, each trough held a story, a reflection of life's enigmatic ebbs and flows.

As the journey began, Morris found solace in the unwavering rhythm of the sea, a metaphor for life's unpredictable currents. The sun rose, casting a golden hue on the tumultuous waves while uncertainty loomed over the horizon. The ocean, like life, presented an undulating canvas of challenges and opportunities. With each passing wave, the MSBR system emerged as a guiding philosophy, a compass amidst the vast uncertainty.

The Mind became the first guiding light on this turbulent voyage, illuminating the path forward. Morris sought refuge in knowledge, recognizing its transformative power amidst the turbulent waters. Even lost at sea, the pursuit of continuous learning became a lifeline, guiding decisions amidst life's tempests. This expanding reservoir of wisdom fortified Morris's resolve to navigate the unpredictable tides.

Yet, amidst the turmoil, the Soul became the beacon of hope—a guiding force amidst the swirling chaos. In the abyss of uncertainty, Morris found solace in the 'Soul' pillar, which embodied the alchemy of ideas and action.

It was the moment ideas took flight, transforming into palpable actions, that steered the course towards uncharted horizons.

However, amid the relentless surges of the sea, the storm tested Morris's resilience and strength. The 'Body' became the anchor, encompassing physical, emotional, and mental well-being. Nurturing the resilience needed to brave the unruly waves and weather the unpredictable storms.

In the heart of the vast expanse, Morris found comfort in the essence of 'Relationships.' The interconnectedness of relationships emerged as a source of hope, even amidst the uncertainty of being adrift. Memories of family, friends, and the threads that wove the fabric of a meaningful life became a lifeline, offering strength, wisdom, and support in the face of the unknown.

And so, amidst the turbulence, the MSBR system encapsulated Morris's journey—a holistic approach to navigating life's rocky waves. Through the synergy of Mind, Soul, Body, and Relationships, Morris transformed into a resilient surfer, lost yet determined, navigating the unpredictable currents with unwavering determination and purpose.

The waves were no longer just challenges; they became a canvas where a life lived fully was painted, where each rise and fall enriched the journey. And as the sun dipped below the horizon, a solitary surfer emerged from the sea, bearing the wisdom of a journey well-surfed.

He made it to shore again.

chapter 5

Journey to Greatness: Setting Goals & Achieving Them

How to set goals that won't burden you

As we move ahead into part two of this book, the guided journaling section, you'll notice that there is a goal-setting exercise for each week. Why? We need to be intentional about balance; it doesn't just happen. And to be intentional, we have to make plans or goals.

So before you go ahead and write down some lofty goals that will only discourage you and burden you, let me review with you a goal-setting theory that you've probably already heard of: **SMART** (Specific, Measurable, Achievable, Relevant, Time-bound) a tool developed by Peter Drucker. Here's something golden to remember before we get going: **A goal that is not sustainable is just wishful thinking.** We want to find the sweet spot between being challenged enough while still being able to keep up our progress for the long haul. Our goals should mean something to us, connecting to a bigger picture that fuels our passion and purpose. It's like taking a big dream and breaking it down into achievable, meaningful steps that excite us. Aligning your goals with what truly matters to you and giving them a deadline gives them purpose and direction. This personalized approach is like setting a roadmap that guides you toward success, making every step count on this fulfilling journey.

S-M-A-R-T Goals

SPECIFIC

What am I going to do ?
Why is this important to me?

MEASUREABLE

How will I measure my success?
How will I know when I've achieved my goal?

ACHIEVABLE

What will I do to achieve this goal?
How will I accomplish it?

RELEVANT

Is this goal worthwhile? How will achieving it help me?
Does this goal fit my values?

TIME-BOUND

When will I accomplish my goal?
How long will I give myself?

S for Specific

In setting specific goals, clearly defining what you want to achieve is essential. This clarity provides a strong foundation for your aspirations. Additionally, writing your goals down in a clear and organized manner is crucial. Documenting them reinforces your commitment and serves as a tangible reference point, ensuring you stay focused and accountable throughout your journey toward achieving them.

Ask yourself this: What am I looking to accomplish? What is my tangible goal?

SPECIFIC GOAL	NON-SPECIFIC GOAL
"I will learn to play the basic chords (A, E, and G) on the acoustic guitar by practicing for at least thirty minutes daily for the next four weeks."	"I want to get better at playing guitar."

EXPLANATION

In the specific goal, it's clear what is to be achieved (learning specific guitar chords), how it will be measured (daily practice for at least thirty minutes), the time frame (the next four weeks), and it's focused on a particular skill (playing guitar chords). This level of specificity makes it easier to track progress and stay motivated.

M for Measurable

Measurable goals enable tracking progress and maintaining focus. It's like a roadmap, guiding you with a defined yardstick, empowering informed decisions, and ensuring consistent progress toward your destination.

Ask yourself this: How much? How many? Identify indicators of progress and set clear criteria for goal achievement. How many times a week? For how long? Which book? With whom?

MEASURABLE GOAL	NON-MEASURABLE GOAL
" In an effort to be more active, I will park my car three blocks away from home every day."	"I want to improve my fitness."

EXPLANATION

The goal "In an effort to be more active, I will park my car three blocks away from home every day" is measurable because it includes specific elements such as the distance (three blocks) and frequency (every day), providing clear criteria for tracking and evaluating progress.

A for Achievable

In the realm of goal setting, achievability is paramount. It's essential to ensure that your goals are not only specific and measurable but also realistic and attainable. This involves a careful consideration of your current resources, skills, and any constraints you might encounter on your journey.

Breaking down larger goals into smaller, manageable tasks or milestones is a strategy that greatly contributes to achievability. When faced with ambitious objectives, this approach mitigates the sense of overwhelm and creates a clear roadmap for progress. By tackling achievable sub-goals one step at a time, you can maintain focus, celebrate incremental successes, and steadily work towards the realization of the larger, overarching goal. It's about making the pursuit feasible and within reach, empowering you to stay motivated and on track throughout the journey.

Ask yourself this: Do I have the resources to succeed with this, time, books? Have I tried this before and failed? If so, what can I do differently?

ACHIEVABLE GOAL	NON-ACHIEVABLE GOAL
"I will work on improving my self-esteem by reading the book "Conversations with Yourself" by Zelig Pliskin twice a week before I go to sleep"	"I want to have perfect self-esteem with unwavering confidence and zero self-doubt by the end of the month"

EXPLANATION

This non-achievable goal is unrealistic because achieving "perfect self-esteem" with "zero self-doubt" in such a short timeframe is highly unlikely. Self-esteem is a complex and deeply ingrained aspect of one's self-concept, and it doesn't follow a linear path to perfection. This goal lacks a realistic assessment of the time and effort required for meaningful self-esteem improvement.

Meanwhile, the achievable self-esteem goal is specific, measurable, achievable, relevant, and time-bound. It outlines practical steps for improving self-esteem and provides a timeframe for assessing progress.

R for Relevant

In the realm of effective goal-setting, ensuring relevance is key. When establishing your goals, it's vital to align them closely with your values, long-term objectives, and the overarching vision you hold for your life or career. This alignment ensures that your efforts are directed toward outcomes that truly matter to you, resonating with the core of who you are and what you aspire to achieve.

By maintaining relevance, you infuse your goals with a sense of purpose and personal significance. Each step you take towards these objectives is a stride towards fulfilling a greater purpose in line with your beliefs and aspirations.

It helps you stay engaged, passionate, and committed throughout the journey as you recognize the meaningful impact these goals can have on your life and the lives of others. Relevance ties your goals to a broader context, providing a solid foundation for your aspirations and reinforcing your motivation to persevere.

Here's the scenario: an individual demonstrates exceptional time management skills, is highly enthusiastic about their career, and currently experiences an imbalance between work and personal life.

RELEVANT GOAL	NOT RELEVANT GOAL
"As I prioritize my career and recognize the importance of maintaining a healthy work-family life balance. I will allocate a weekly slot in my schedule for a lunch date with my spouse."	"I will dedicate an additional hour daily to researching methods for self-motivation in the workplace."

EXPLANATION

This goal is relevant to the individual because it addresses the recognized imbalance between work and personal life. Prioritizing a weekly lunch date with their spouse aligns with the individual's values of maintaining a healthy work-family life balance, contributing to overall well-being and life satisfaction.

T for Time-bound

Setting a clear time frame or deadline for a goal is imperative in driving progress and maintaining focused efforts. A time-bound goal should encompass a defined period or a target end date, instilling a sense of urgency that motivates decisive action. Especially for more significant objectives, breaking them down into manageable chunks with their timelines can enhance efficiency. This approach not only establishes a realistic end date but also aids in staying on course and effectively managing the goal.

To institute a time frame for a goal, a pivotal question must be addressed: Defining a specific date or timeframe by which the goal will be accomplished establishes a clear endpoint to strive for. This deadline injects urgency and accountability into the goal-setting process, compelling consistent actions toward its realization. Additionally, considering what can be accomplished today within this time frame is equally essential for maintaining momentum and meeting objectives efficiently.

Ask yourself this: Does my goal have a deadline?
When do you want to achieve your goal?

TIME-BOUND GOAL	NOT A TIME-BOUND GOAL
I want to learn conversational Spanish within six months by devoting thirty minutes a day to language learning.	I want to learn a new language.

EXPLANATION

Let's look at the goal on the right that is not time-bound. It lacks a specific timeframe or deadline. While it's clear that the person wants to learn a new language, there's no indication of when they aim to achieve this.

In contrast, the goal on the left specifies a clear timeframe (six months) and outlines the frequency (thirty minutes a day) for working towards the goal. This provides a specific timeframe for achieving the goal, making it more actionable and measurable. This is the purpose of the calender in the journal.

EVEN MORE EXAMPLES OF SMART GOALS

This is a really strong statement, but I think it's true: the success of your journey hinges on the types of goals that you set up for yourself. So we really have to get this right.

So, were going to give you even more examples of the types of goals that you can set up for yourself that will help you bring balance to the four pillars of your life:

MIND

The overarching theme of your goals for 'MIND' will be around acquiring knowledge and training your mind to think positively and remove negativity.

1 Enhancing Time Management Skills:

I know that if I increase my time management skills, I'll be able to learn more. So, in order to do this, I am committing to reading "The 7 Habits of Highly Effective People" by Stephen Covey twice a week for thirty minutes, first thing in the morning, as I have my morning coffee. This deliberate practice aims to refine my time management abilities.

2 Understand my Emotional Landscape:

To delve deeper into understanding my emotional landscape, I've integrated listening to Chaim Levy's insightful podcast "Noise to Music" into my commute once a week (Shoutout to my podcast!). This intentional choice enriches my emotional understanding during transit times.

3 Expand my Worldview through Study:

On Friday nights, I prioritized expanding my worldview and gaining insight into life by dedicating time to studying the Bible. This practice broadens my perspective and enriches my understanding of life's complexities.

4 Learn how to manage my anger:

Knowing that I have a tendency towards inappropriate expressions of anger, I want to take steps toward addressing it by acquiring new skills and perspectives. I commit to spending Wednesday nights from 8:30 pm to 9:30 pm reading the book, "Anger: The Inner Teacher" by Zelig Pliskin. This dedicated effort is geared toward comprehending and managing anger reactions, increasing my emotional intelligence.

Scout Your Emotional Landscape. Imagine each situation in your life is like a broad landscape that can only be properly analyzed if you hike a mountain and look at it from a higher level. Look down at your emotional landscape and judge if it is a good place for you.

SOUL

The overarching theme of your goals for 'SOUL' is to create circumstances for impactful actions.

1 Peace & relaxation first thing in the morning.

In my quest to deepen my spiritual connection, I've committed to starting my Mondays and Thursdays by waking up at 6:30 AM instead of 7:00 AM so that I have the extra time to engage in meditation or prayer, which will set a peaceful tone for my day ahead.

2 Replace negative speech with Positive speech:

Recognizing the impact of negative speech, I've marked Wednesday morning as a time when I will make a conscious effort to refrain from speaking negatively about others, fostering a more positive and uplifting environment.

3 Go on a gratitude walk twice a week:

In recognition of all the beauty that nature has to offer, every Tuesday and Thursday, I will park my car at Nelson's Park. This intentional walk allows me to reflect on and appreciate the things I am thankful for each day, whether it's the beauty of nature, the unwavering support of loved ones, or simply the gift of mobility and the ability to relish the outdoors.

4 Spend the evening writing in my journal

Every night, I will spend time journaling my thoughts and feelings; this will help organize my mind, reduce stress, and bring clarity to my emotions.

BODY

The overarching theme of your goals for 'BODY' is to fortify your vessel or improve the strength and overall health of your body.

1 Sunday Morning Cycling:

This Sunday morning, I will go cycling with a friend, combining physical activity and social interaction for a positive start to the week.

2 Reduced Screen time for better sleep:

To enhance my sleep quality and promote positive morning thoughts, I've decided not to charge my phone next to my bed overnight. This practice will help me wake up without immediately looking at my phone, fostering a more positive mindset.

3 Eliminate sugary beverages

I've committed to cutting out sugar-based beverages entirely during my work hours on Monday and supplementing with water. This shift in my beverage choice will contribute to a healthier lifestyle.

4 Relaxing Coffee & Reflective Journaling:

I've scheduled a peaceful ritual on Tuesday evenings after work. I'll take some time to enjoy a cup of coffee and write in my journal, allowing space for self-reflection and mental organization.

RELATIONSHIPS

The overarching theme of your goals for 'RELATIONSHIPS' is to build relationships that are healthy and grounded in love and respect.

1 Healing from past hurt

Recognizing the impact of past relationship hurt, I've committed to seek therapy. This Monday, during my lunch period, I will research two local therapists and contact them for an initial appointment. This step is essential in processing and letting go of the pain, allowing for emotional healing.

2 Spend quality time with my children:

Acknowledging the need for more meaningful moments with my children, I'm setting aside dedicated time to have dinner together as a family once a week, starting this Friday. For the ensuing weeks, the night will have to be discussed with the rest of the family to accommodate everyone's schedules. This effort aims to strengthen our bond and create cherished memories.

3 Go on a special date night

With the understanding that my relationship with my spouse requires intentionality and quality time spent, I will book us in for a special dinner at my spouse's favorite restaurant for Thursday night. This thoughtful gesture is a way to show appreciation and strengthen our relationship through shared experiences.

4 Connect with my best friend

I plan to give my best friend a call during my lunch break on Wednesday just to say "hello." This small act of reaching out is aimed at nurturing and maintaining our friendship, ensuring that our connection remains strong and valued.

Am I ready to turn the page?

"The Spiraling Sketchbook"

In a town where imagination painted the horizon lived a young artist named Oliver. Armed with a sketchbook and a pencil, he set out on a creative journey that would shape his artistic destiny.

At first, Oliver's sketches were simple, tracing the outlines of his surroundings. Yet, with each page turned, he sought to challenge himself with more intricate designs and daring concepts. The sketchbook, once filled with basic drawings, began to transform into a testament to his evolving skills.

As Oliver flipped through the pages, he realized that the joy wasn't just in the finished sketches but in the process of growth. The satisfaction of conquering a new challenge fueled his desire to repeat the cycle, each repetition reaching for higher goals.

Embracing the concept of a spiraling sketchbook, Oliver set out to create more complex and ambitious drawings. The once-static sketches now seemed to dance with life, each swirl and curve representing the determination to surpass previous limitations.

Are You Ready for a New Challenge?

The Spiraling Sketchbook parable invites us to view our goals as a continuous, upward spiral. Oliver's artistic journey encourages us not only to repeat and refine but also to elevate our aspirations with each cycle. It teaches us that the sketchbook of life is boundless, with each page presenting an opportunity to set new, higher goals and marvel at the ever-expanding canvas of our potential.

Knowing when to progress to the next level of a goal is crucial for sustainable growth. Here are some signs that you might be ready to take your habit to the next level:

Ask Yourself This:

- Is it time to change any of the goals?
- Did I take upon myself too much? How do I break it down into "Bite-Size" pieces?
- What strengths or weaknesses did I discover about myself?
- Is there a goal I can set for next week that is part of my overall journey, will have an impact, and is achievable?

part 2
EMBARKING ON THE TRAIL OF LIFE

How to use this Journal

Explore. Reflect. Write

Each week, you'll be given blank journaling pages to write whatever you'd like. Having a regular time set aside for journaling can have immense holistic benefits, as you already know from reading chapter four. Now, we're going to give you a few tips to help you get the most out of your journaling experience:

CREATE A ROUTINE Set aside a specific time and space that you journal; this might be daily or the same time and place every week.

CONCENTRATE ON REFLECTION Use your journal to reflect on significant events or moments in your life. Think about how these experiences have shaped you and what you've learned from them.

LOOK BACK ON PREVIOUS ENTRIES Review your entries periodically to identify patterns or changes in your thoughts, behaviors and feelings. This can help you understand your growth and areas where you want to improve.

Paths to Progress

Each week, you'll have a goal-setting sheet where you can jot down goals for each of your MSBR[s].

In addition, we've added a section called "General Stuff to do this week." While these tasks may not necessarily be focused on growth, they are crucial for staying organized and on track.

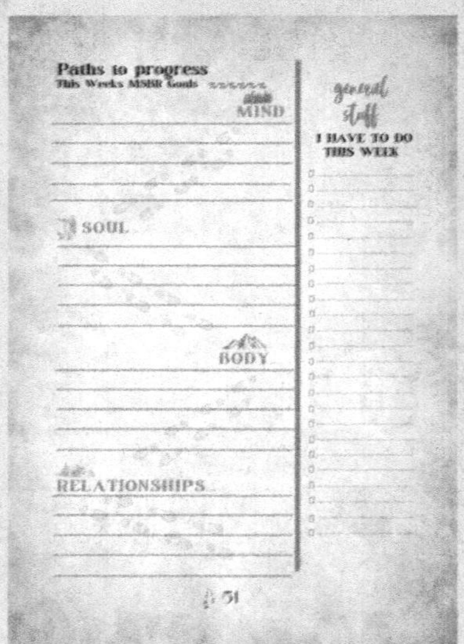

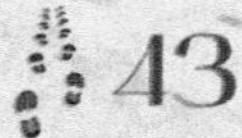

Weekly Goal Tracker

Achieve your Goals with this simple weekly planner.

This filled-out weekly planner marks the start of our positivity momentum. It's achievable, spaced out, and clearly outlined. What's the aim? To initiate a 'Wave of Positivity.' Each day holds specific, timed, and diverse goals across all four pillars. As you progress next week, you will assess whether you need to add another step to your goal and ride out this wave toward harmony. Just to give you some ideas, **I've included an example of a filled-in weekly goal tracker. Turn the page to check it out!**

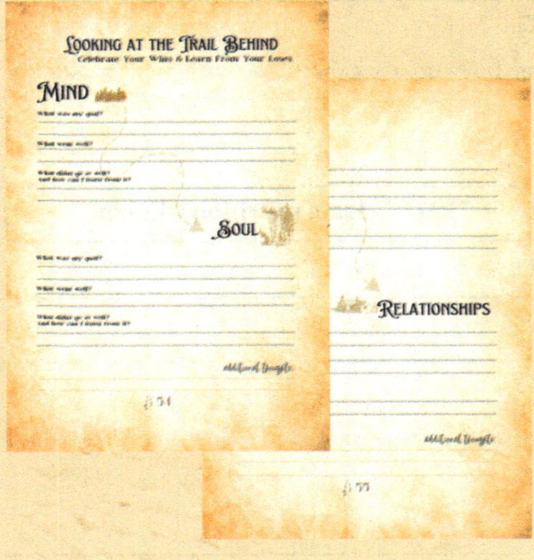

Looking at the Trail Behind

Each week, you'll have three questions to answer as you reflect on the goals that you set for yourself at the beginning of the week.

1. What was my goal?
2. What went well?
3. What didn't go so well? And how can I learn from it?

Why are these questions so important?

During my teaching career, I've seen so many of my students fall into the habit of setting goals, not achieving the hoped-for outcome, and then giving up on their efforts toward self-growth. This is nothing short of a tragedy and can be easily avoided by taking the time to step back and look at what went well and what didn't go so well.

By learning to celebrate your wins and learn from your losses, you'll become more patient with yourself and your lifelong process of self-growth.

SUNDAY

TIME	GOAL / TASK	M/S/B/R	TIME	GOAL / TASK	M/S/B/R
☐ 8AM	go for a walk	S	☐ 11PM	reduce screen time	B
☐			☐		
☐			☐		
☐			☐		

MONDAY

TIME	GOAL / TASK	M/S/B/R	TIME	GOAL / TASK	M/S/B/R
☐ 8AM	coffee with a friend	R	☐ 7PM	Therapy session for inner healing	S
☐			☐		
☐			☐		
☐			☐		

TUESDAY

TIME	GOAL / TASK	M/S/B/R	TIME	GOAL / TASK	M/S/B/R
☐ 10AM	morning meditation	M	☐ 7PM	Eat a nutritious dinner	B
☐ 12PM	go for a jog over lunch hour	B	☐		
☐			☐		
☐			☐		

WEDNESDAY

TIME	GOAL / TASK	M/S/B/R	TIME	GOAL / TASK	M/S/B/R
☐ 7AM	call mom before class	R	☐ 8PM	Read Book: 7 Habits	M
☐			☐		
☐			☐		
☐			☐		

THURSDAY

TIME	GOAL / TASK	M/S/B/R	TIME	GOAL / TASK	M/S/B/R
☐ 7AM	make myself a smoothie for breakfast	B	☐ 8PM	Study for test	M
☐			☐		
☐			☐		
☐			☐		

Check out this week's
Inspiring recording!
date:
THE 90-DAY
MSBR Journal
WEEK 1

Identify what mindset you would like to work on.

What self-care activity would make the greatest impact?

Can you identify a relationship that needs more love?

What actions can I take to rewire my inner being?

EXPLORE
reflect & WRITE

EXPLORE
reflect & WRITE

Paths to progress

This Week's MSBR Goals

MIND...

SOUL...

BODY..

RELATIONSHIPS....

general stuff

I HAVE TO DO THIS WEEK

- [ ]
- [ ]
- [ ]
- [ ]
- [ ]
- [ ]
- [ ]
- [ ]
- [ ]
- [ ]
- [ ]
- [ ]
- [ ]
- [ ]
- [ ]
- [ ]
- [ ]
- [ ]
- [ ]
- [ ]
- [ ]
- [ ]
- [ ]
- [ ]

SUNDAY

TIME	GOAL / TASK	M/S/B/R
☐		
☐		
☐		
☐		
☐		
☐		

TIME	GOAL / TASK	M/S/B/R
☐		
☐		
☐		
☐		
☐		
☐		

MONDAY

TIME	GOAL / TASK	M/S/B/R
☐		
☐		
☐		
☐		
☐		
☐		

TIME	GOAL / TASK	M/S/B/R
☐		
☐		
☐		
☐		
☐		
☐		

TUESDAY

TIME	GOAL / TASK	M/S/B/R
☐		
☐		
☐		
☐		
☐		
☐		

TIME	GOAL / TASK	M/S/B/R
☐		
☐		
☐		
☐		
☐		
☐		

WEDNESDAY

TIME	GOAL / TASK	M/S/B/R
☐		
☐		
☐		
☐		
☐		
☐		

TIME	GOAL / TASK	M/S/B/R
☐		
☐		
☐		
☐		
☐		
☐		

THURSDAY

TIME	GOAL / TASK	M/S/B/R
☐		
☐		
☐		
☐		
☐		
☐		

TIME	GOAL / TASK	M/S/B/R
☐		
☐		
☐		
☐		
☐		
☐		

FRIDAY

TIME	GOAL / TASK	M/S/B/R
☐		
☐		
☐		
☐		
☐		
☐		

TIME	GOAL / TASK	M/S/B/R
☐		
☐		
☐		
☐		
☐		
☐		

SATURDAY

TIME	GOAL / TASK	M/S/B/R
☐		
☐		
☐		
☐		
☐		
☐		

TIME	GOAL / TASK	M/S/B/R
☐		
☐		
☐		
☐		
☐		
☐		

MY INSIGHT OF THE WEEK:

Looking at the Trail Behind

Celebrate Your Wins & Learn From Your Loses

Mind

What was my goal?

What went well?

What didnt go so well?
And how can I learn from it?

Soul

What was my goal?

What went well?

What didnt go so well?
And how can I learn from it?

additional thoughts:

Body

What was my goal?

What went well?

What didn't go so well?
And how can I learn from it?

Relationships

What was my goal?

What went well?

What didn't go so well?
And how can I learn from it?

additional thoughts:

Check out this weeks
Inspiring recording!
date:
THE 90-DAY
MSBR Journal
WEEK
2

EXPLORE
reflect & WRITE

EXPLORE
reflect & WRITE

EXPLORE
reflect & WRITE

EXPLORE
reflect & WRITE

Paths to progress

This Week's MSBR Goals

MIND...

SOUL...

BODY..

RELATIONSHIPS....

general stuff

I HAVE TO DO THIS WEEK

SUNDAY

TIME	GOAL / TASK	M/S/B/R
☐		
☐		
☐		
☐		
☐		
☐		

TIME	GOAL / TASK	M/S/B/R
☐		
☐		
☐		
☐		
☐		
☐		

MONDAY

TIME	GOAL / TASK	M/S/B/R
☐		
☐		
☐		
☐		
☐		
☐		

TIME	GOAL / TASK	M/S/B/R
☐		
☐		
☐		
☐		
☐		
☐		

TUESDAY

TIME	GOAL / TASK	M/S/B/R
☐		
☐		
☐		
☐		
☐		
☐		

TIME	GOAL / TASK	M/S/B/R
☐		
☐		
☐		
☐		
☐		
☐		

WEDNESDAY

TIME	GOAL / TASK	M/S/B/R
☐		
☐		
☐		
☐		
☐		
☐		

TIME	GOAL / TASK	M/S/B/R
☐		
☐		
☐		
☐		
☐		
☐		

THURSDAY

TIME	GOAL / TASK	M/S/B/R
☐		
☐		
☐		
☐		
☐		
☐		

TIME	GOAL / TASK	M/S/B/R
☐		
☐		
☐		
☐		
☐		
☐		

FRIDAY

TIME	GOAL / TASK	M/S/B/R
☐		
☐		
☐		
☐		
☐		
☐		

TIME	GOAL / TASK	M/S/B/R
☐		
☐		
☐		
☐		
☐		
☐		

SATURDAY

TIME	GOAL / TASK	M/S/B/R
☐		
☐		
☐		
☐		
☐		
☐		

TIME	GOAL / TASK	M/S/B/R
☐		
☐		
☐		
☐		
☐		
☐		

MY INSIGHT OF THE WEEK:

Looking at the Trail Behind

Celebrate Your Wins & Learn From Your Loses

Mind

What was my goal?

What went well?

What didn't go so well?
And how can I learn from it?

Soul

What was my goal?

What went well?

What didn't go so well?
And how can I learn from it?

Body

What was my goal?

What went well?

What didn't go so well?
And how can I learn from it?

Relationships

What was my goal?

What went well?

What didnt go so well?
And how can I learn from it?

additional thoughts:

Check out this week's
Inspiring recording!
date:
THE 90-DAY
MSBR Journal
WEEK 3

EXPLORE
reflect & WRITE

EXPLORE
reflect & WRITE

EXPLORE
reflect & WRITE

EXPLORE
reflect & WRITE

Paths to progress

This Week's MSBR Goals

MIND...

SOUL...

BODY..

RELATIONSHIPS....

general stuff

I HAVE TO DO THIS WEEK

- [ ]
- [ ]
- [ ]
- [ ]
- [ ]
- [ ]
- [ ]
- [ ]
- [ ]
- [ ]
- [ ]
- [ ]
- [ ]
- [ ]
- [ ]
- [ ]
- [ ]
- [ ]
- [ ]
- [ ]
- [ ]
- [ ]
- [ ]
- [ ]

SUNDAY

TIME	GOAL / TASK	M/S/B/R	TIME	GOAL / TASK	M/S/B/R
☐			☐		
☐			☐		
☐			☐		
☐			☐		
☐			☐		
☐			☐		

MONDAY

TIME	GOAL / TASK	M/S/B/R	TIME	GOAL / TASK	M/S/B/R
☐			☐		
☐			☐		
☐			☐		
☐			☐		
☐			☐		
☐			☐		

TUESDAY

TIME	GOAL / TASK	M/S/B/R	TIME	GOAL / TASK	M/S/B/R
☐			☐		
☐			☐		
☐			☐		
☐			☐		
☐			☐		
☐			☐		

WEDNESDAY

TIME	GOAL / TASK	M/S/B/R	TIME	GOAL / TASK	M/S/B/R
☐			☐		
☐			☐		
☐			☐		
☐			☐		
☐			☐		
☐			☐		

THURSDAY

TIME	GOAL / TASK	M/S/B/R
☐		
☐		
☐		
☐		
☐		
☐		

TIME	GOAL / TASK	M/S/B/R
☐		
☐		
☐		
☐		
☐		
☐		

FRIDAY

TIME	GOAL / TASK	M/S/B/R
☐		
☐		
☐		
☐		
☐		
☐		

TIME	GOAL / TASK	M/S/B/R
☐		
☐		
☐		
☐		
☐		
☐		

SATURDAY

TIME	GOAL / TASK	M/S/B/R
☐		
☐		
☐		
☐		
☐		
☐		

TIME	GOAL / TASK	M/S/B/R
☐		
☐		
☐		
☐		
☐		
☐		

MY INSIGHT OF THE WEEK:

Looking at the Trail Behind

Celebrate Your Wins & Learn From Your Loses

Mind

What was my goal?

What went well?

What didnt go so well?
And how can I learn from it?

Soul

What was my goal?

What went well?

What didnt go so well?
And how can I learn from it?

additional thoughts:

Body

What was my goal?

What went well?

What didn't go so well?
And how can I learn from it?

Relationships

What was my goal?

What went well?

What didn't go so well?
And how can I learn from it?

additional thoughts:

Check out this weeks
Inspiring recording!
date:
THE 90-DAY
MSBR Journal
WEEK
4

EXPLORE
reflect & WRITE

EXPLORE
reflect & WRITE

EXPLORE
reflect & WRITE

EXPLORE
reflect & WRITE

Paths to progress

This Week's MSBR Goals

MIND...

SOUL...

BODY..

RELATIONSHIPS....

general stuff

I HAVE TO DO THIS WEEK

- [ ]
- [ ]
- [ ]
- [ ]
- [ ]
- [ ]
- [ ]
- [ ]
- [ ]
- [ ]
- [ ]
- [ ]
- [ ]
- [ ]
- [ ]
- [ ]
- [ ]
- [ ]
- [ ]
- [ ]
- [ ]
- [ ]
- [ ]
- [ ]

SUNDAY

TIME	GOAL / TASK	M/S/B/R	TIME	GOAL / TASK	M/S/B/R
☐			☐		
☐			☐		
☐			☐		
☐			☐		
☐			☐		
☐			☐		

MONDAY

TIME	GOAL / TASK	M/S/B/R	TIME	GOAL / TASK	M/S/B/R
☐			☐		
☐			☐		
☐			☐		
☐			☐		
☐			☐		
☐			☐		

TUESDAY

TIME	GOAL / TASK	M/S/B/R	TIME	GOAL / TASK	M/S/B/R
☐			☐		
☐			☐		
☐			☐		
☐			☐		
☐			☐		
☐			☐		

WEDNESDAY

TIME	GOAL / TASK	M/S/B/R	TIME	GOAL / TASK	M/S/B/R
☐			☐		
☐			☐		
☐			☐		
☐			☐		
☐			☐		
☐			☐		

THURSDAY

TIME	GOAL / TASK	M/S/B/R
☐		
☐		
☐		
☐		
☐		
☐		

TIME	GOAL / TASK	M/S/B/R
☐		
☐		
☐		
☐		
☐		
☐		

FRIDAY

TIME	GOAL / TASK	M/S/B/R
☐		
☐		
☐		
☐		
☐		
☐		

TIME	GOAL / TASK	M/S/B/R
☐		
☐		
☐		
☐		
☐		
☐		

SATURDAY

TIME	GOAL / TASK	M/S/B/R
☐		
☐		
☐		
☐		
☐		
☐		

TIME	GOAL / TASK	M/S/B/R
☐		
☐		
☐		
☐		
☐		
☐		

MY INSIGHT OF THE WEEK:

Looking at the Trail Behind

Celebrate Your Wins & Learn From Your Loses

Mind

What was my goal?

What went well?

What didn't go so well?
And how can I learn from it?

Soul

What was my goal?

What went well?

What didn't go so well?
And how can I learn from it?

additional thoughts:

Body

What was my goal?

What went well?

**What didn't go so well?
And how can I learn from it?**

Relationships

What was my goal?

What went well?

**What didn't go so well?
And how can I learn from it?**

additional thoughts:

Check out this week's
Inspiring recording!
date:
THE 90-DAY
MSBR Journal
WEEK 5

EXPLORE
reflect & WRITE

EXPLORE
reflect & WRITE

EXPLORE
reflect &
WRITE

EXPLORE
reflect & WRITE

Paths to progress

This Weeks MSBR Goals

MIND...

SOUL...

BODY..

RELATIONSHIPS....

general stuff

I HAVE TO DO THIS WEEK

SUNDAY

TIME	GOAL / TASK	M/S/B/R	TIME	GOAL / TASK	M/S/B/R
☐			☐		
☐			☐		
☐			☐		
☐			☐		
☐			☐		
☐			☐		

MONDAY

TIME	GOAL / TASK	M/S/B/R	TIME	GOAL / TASK	M/S/B/R
☐			☐		
☐			☐		
☐			☐		
☐			☐		
☐			☐		
☐			☐		

TUESDAY

TIME	GOAL / TASK	M/S/B/R	TIME	GOAL / TASK	M/S/B/R
☐			☐		
☐			☐		
☐			☐		
☐			☐		
☐			☐		
☐			☐		

WEDNESDAY

TIME	GOAL / TASK	M/S/B/R	TIME	GOAL / TASK	M/S/B/R
☐			☐		
☐			☐		
☐			☐		
☐			☐		
☐			☐		
☐			☐		

THURSDAY

TIME	GOAL / TASK	M/S/B/R
☐		
☐		
☐		
☐		
☐		
☐		

TIME	GOAL / TASK	M/S/B/R
☐		
☐		
☐		
☐		
☐		
☐		

FRIDAY

TIME	GOAL / TASK	M/S/B/R
☐		
☐		
☐		
☐		
☐		
☐		

TIME	GOAL / TASK	M/S/B/R
☐		
☐		
☐		
☐		
☐		
☐		

SATURDAY

TIME	GOAL / TASK	M/S/B/R
☐		
☐		
☐		
☐		
☐		
☐		

TIME	GOAL / TASK	M/S/B/R
☐		
☐		
☐		
☐		
☐		
☐		

MY INSIGHT OF THE WEEK:

Looking at the Trail Behind

Celebrate Your Wins & Learn From Your Loses

Mind

What was my goal?

What went well?

What didn't go so well?
And how can I learn from it?

Soul

What was my goal?

What went well?

What didn't go so well?
And how can I learn from it?

additional thoughts:

Body

What was my goal?

What went well?

What didnt go so well?
And how can I learn from it?

Relationships

What was my goal?

What went well?

What didnt go so well?
And how can I learn from it?

additional thoughts:

Check out this weeks
Inspiring recording!
date:
THE 90-DAY
MSBR Journal
WEEK
6

We're at the halfway mark! Pause and journal about your journey. Celebrate your progress, recognize lessons learned, and ignite the inspiration for the road ahead.

Compare your goals from Week 1 with your current reality. How have your progressed?

Have you discovered new strengths or found ways to address weaknesses?

How can you incorporate moments of presence into your daily routine?

How does prioritizing self-care contribute to your overall resilience and well-being?

EXPLORE
reflect & WRITE

Paths to progress
This Weeks MSBR Goals

MIND...

SOUL...

BODY..

RELATIONSHIPS....

general stuff

I HAVE TO DO THIS WEEK

- [ ]
- [ ]
- [ ]
- [ ]
- [ ]
- [ ]
- [ ]
- [ ]
- [ ]
- [ ]
- [ ]
- [ ]
- [ ]
- [ ]
- [ ]
- [ ]
- [ ]
- [ ]
- [ ]
- [ ]
- [ ]
- [ ]
- [ ]
- [ ]

Paths to progress

This Week's MSBR Goals

MIND...

SOUL...

BODY..

RELATIONSHIPS....

general stuff

I HAVE TO DO THIS WEEK

- [ ]
- [ ]
- [ ]
- [ ]
- [ ]
- [ ]
- [ ]
- [ ]
- [ ]
- [ ]
- [ ]
- [ ]
- [ ]
- [ ]
- [ ]
- [ ]
- [ ]
- [ ]
- [ ]
- [ ]
- [ ]
- [ ]
- [ ]
- [ ]

SUNDAY

TIME	GOAL / TASK	M/S/B/R
	☐	
	☐	
	☐	
	☐	
	☐	
	☐	

TIME	GOAL / TASK	M/S/B/R
	☐	
	☐	
	☐	
	☐	
	☐	
	☐	

MONDAY

TIME	GOAL / TASK	M/S/B/R
	☐	
	☐	
	☐	
	☐	
	☐	
	☐	

TIME	GOAL / TASK	M/S/B/R
	☐	
	☐	
	☐	
	☐	
	☐	
	☐	

TUESDAY

TIME	GOAL / TASK	M/S/B/R
	☐	
	☐	
	☐	
	☐	
	☐	
	☐	

TIME	GOAL / TASK	M/S/B/R
	☐	
	☐	
	☐	
	☐	
	☐	
	☐	

WEDNESDAY

TIME	GOAL / TASK	M/S/B/R
	☐	
	☐	
	☐	
	☐	
	☐	
	☐	

TIME	GOAL / TASK	M/S/B/R
	☐	
	☐	
	☐	
	☐	
	☐	
	☐	

THURSDAY

TIME	GOAL / TASK	M/S/B/R
☐		
☐		
☐		
☐		
☐		
☐		

TIME	GOAL / TASK	M/S/B/R
☐		
☐		
☐		
☐		
☐		
☐		

FRIDAY

TIME	GOAL / TASK	M/S/B/R
☐		
☐		
☐		
☐		
☐		
☐		

TIME	GOAL / TASK	M/S/B/R
☐		
☐		
☐		
☐		
☐		
☐		

SATURDAY

TIME	GOAL / TASK	M/S/B/R
☐		
☐		
☐		
☐		
☐		
☐		

TIME	GOAL / TASK	M/S/B/R
☐		
☐		
☐		
☐		
☐		
☐		

MY INSIGHT OF THE WEEK:

Looking at the Trail Behind

Celebrate Your Wins & Learn From Your Loses

Mind

What was my goal?

What went well?

What didn't go so well?
And how can I learn from it?

Soul

What was my goal?

What went well?

What didn't go so well?
And how can I learn from it?

additional thoughts:

Body

What was my goal?

What went well?

What didn't go so well?
And how can I learn from it?

Relationships

What was my goal?

What went well?

What didn't go so well?
And how can I learn from it?

additional thoughts:

Check out this week's
Inspiring recording!
date:
THE 90-DAY
MSBR Journal
WEEK 7

EXPLORE
reflect & WRITE

EXPLORE
reflect & WRITE

EXPLORE
reflect & WRITE

EXPLORE
reflect & WRITE

Paths to progress

This Weeks MSBR Goals

MIND...

SOUL...

BODY...

RELATIONSHIPS....

general stuff

I HAVE TO DO THIS WEEK

- [ ]
- [ ]
- [ ]
- [ ]
- [ ]
- [ ]
- [ ]
- [ ]
- [ ]
- [ ]
- [ ]
- [ ]
- [ ]
- [ ]
- [ ]
- [ ]
- [ ]
- [ ]
- [ ]
- [ ]
- [ ]
- [ ]
- [ ]
- [ ]

SUNDAY

TIME	GOAL / TASK	M/S/B/R	TIME	GOAL / TASK	M/S/B/R
☐			☐		
☐			☐		
☐			☐		
☐			☐		
☐			☐		
☐			☐		

MONDAY

TIME	GOAL / TASK	M/S/B/R	TIME	GOAL / TASK	M/S/B/R
☐			☐		
☐			☐		
☐			☐		
☐			☐		
☐			☐		
☐			☐		

TUESDAY

TIME	GOAL / TASK	M/S/B/R	TIME	GOAL / TASK	M/S/B/R
☐			☐		
☐			☐		
☐			☐		
☐			☐		
☐			☐		
☐			☐		

WEDNESDAY

TIME	GOAL / TASK	M/S/B/R	TIME	GOAL / TASK	M/S/B/R
☐			☐		
☐			☐		
☐			☐		
☐			☐		
☐			☐		
☐			☐		

THURSDAY

TIME	GOAL / TASK	M/S/B/R
☐		
☐		
☐		
☐		
☐		
☐		

TIME	GOAL / TASK	M/S/B/R
☐		
☐		
☐		
☐		
☐		
☐		

FRIDAY

TIME	GOAL / TASK	M/S/B/R
☐		
☐		
☐		
☐		
☐		
☐		

TIME	GOAL / TASK	M/S/B/R
☐		
☐		
☐		
☐		
☐		
☐		

SATURDAY

TIME	GOAL / TASK	M/S/B/R
☐		
☐		
☐		
☐		
☐		
☐		

TIME	GOAL / TASK	M/S/B/R
☐		
☐		
☐		
☐		
☐		
☐		

MY INSIGHT OF THE WEEK:

Looking at the Trail Behind

Celebrate Your Wins & Learn From Your Loses

Mind

What was my goal?

What went well?

What didnt go so well?
And how can I learn from it?

Soul

What was my goal?

What went well?

What didnt go so well?
And how can I learn from it?

additional thoughts:

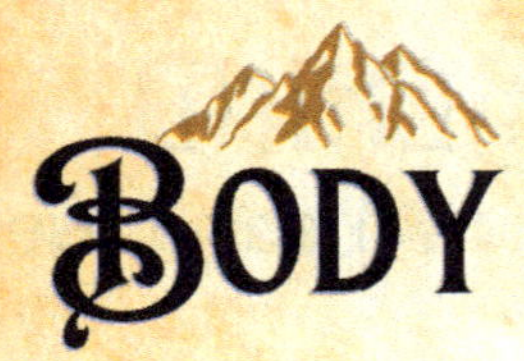

Body

What was my goal?

What went well?

What didn't go so well?
And how can I learn from it?

Relationships

What was my goal?

What went well?

What didn't go so well?
And how can I learn from it?

additional thoughts:

Check out this weeks
Inspiring recording!
date:
THE 90-DAY
MSBR Journal
WEEK
8

EXPLORE
reflect & WRITE

EXPLORE
reflect & WRITE

EXPLORE
reflect & WRITE

EXPLORE
reflect & WRITE

Paths to progress

This Week's MSBR Goals

MIND...

SOUL...

BODY..

RELATIONSHIPS....

general stuff

I HAVE TO DO THIS WEEK

- ☐
- ☐
- ☐
- ☐
- ☐
- ☐
- ☐
- ☐
- ☐
- ☐
- ☐
- ☐
- ☐
- ☐
- ☐
- ☐
- ☐
- ☐
- ☐
- ☐
- ☐
- ☐
- ☐
- ☐

TIME	GOAL / TASK	M/S/B/R
☐		
☐		
☐		
☐		
☐		
☐		

SUNDAY

TIME	GOAL / TASK	M/S/B/R
☐		
☐		
☐		
☐		
☐		
☐		

TIME	GOAL / TASK	M/S/B/R
☐		
☐		
☐		
☐		
☐		
☐		

MONDAY

TIME	GOAL / TASK	M/S/B/R
☐		
☐		
☐		
☐		
☐		
☐		

TIME	GOAL / TASK	M/S/B/R
☐		
☐		
☐		
☐		
☐		
☐		

TUESDAY

TIME	GOAL / TASK	M/S/B/R
☐		
☐		
☐		
☐		
☐		
☐		

TIME	GOAL / TASK	M/S/B/R
☐		
☐		
☐		
☐		
☐		
☐		

WEDNESDAY

TIME	GOAL / TASK	M/S/B/R
☐		
☐		
☐		
☐		
☐		
☐		

THURSDAY

TIME	GOAL / TASK	M/S/B/R
☐		
☐		
☐		
☐		
☐		
☐		

TIME	GOAL / TASK	M/S/B/R
☐		
☐		
☐		
☐		
☐		
☐		

FRIDAY

TIME	GOAL / TASK	M/S/B/R
☐		
☐		
☐		
☐		
☐		
☐		

TIME	GOAL / TASK	M/S/B/R
☐		
☐		
☐		
☐		
☐		
☐		

SATURDAY

TIME	GOAL / TASK	M/S/B/R
☐		
☐		
☐		
☐		
☐		
☐		

TIME	GOAL / TASK	M/S/B/R
☐		
☐		
☐		
☐		
☐		
☐		

MY INSIGHT OF THE WEEK:

Looking at the Trail Behind

Celebrate Your Wins & Learn From Your Loses

Mind

What was my goal?

What went well?

What didnt go so well?
And how can I learn from it?

Soul

What was my goal?

What went well?

What didnt go so well?
And how can I learn from it?

additional thoughts:

Body

What was my goal?

What went well?

What didn't go so well?
And how can I learn from it?

Relationships

What was my goal?

What went well?

What didn't go so well?
And how can I learn from it?

additional thoughts:

Check out this week's
Inspiring recording!
date:
THE 90-DAY
MSBR Journal
WEEK 9

EXPLORE
reflect & WRITE

EXPLORE
reflect & WRITE

EXPLORE
reflect & WRITE

EXPLORE
reflect & WRITE

Paths to progress

This Weeks MSBR Goals

MIND...

SOUL...

BODY..

RELATIONSHIPS....

general stuff

I HAVE TO DO THIS WEEK

SUNDAY

TIME	GOAL / TASK	M/S/B/R	TIME	GOAL / TASK	M/S/B/R
☐			☐		
☐			☐		
☐			☐		
☐			☐		
☐			☐		
☐			☐		

MONDAY

TIME	GOAL / TASK	M/S/B/R	TIME	GOAL / TASK	M/S/B/R
☐			☐		
☐			☐		
☐			☐		
☐			☐		
☐			☐		
☐			☐		

TUESDAY

TIME	GOAL / TASK	M/S/B/R	TIME	GOAL / TASK	M/S/B/R
☐			☐		
☐			☐		
☐			☐		
☐			☐		
☐			☐		
☐			☐		

WEDNESDAY

TIME	GOAL / TASK	M/S/B/R	TIME	GOAL / TASK	M/S/B/R
☐			☐		
☐			☐		
☐			☐		
☐			☐		
☐			☐		
☐			☐		

THURSDAY

TIME	GOAL / TASK	M/S/B/R
☐		
☐		
☐		
☐		
☐		
☐		

TIME	GOAL / TASK	M/S/B/R
☐		
☐		
☐		
☐		
☐		
☐		

FRIDAY

TIME	GOAL / TASK	M/S/B/R
☐		
☐		
☐		
☐		
☐		
☐		

TIME	GOAL / TASK	M/S/B/R
☐		
☐		
☐		
☐		
☐		
☐		

SATURDAY

TIME	GOAL / TASK	M/S/B/R
☐		
☐		
☐		
☐		
☐		
☐		

TIME	GOAL / TASK	M/S/B/R
☐		
☐		
☐		
☐		
☐		
☐		

MY INSIGHT OF THE WEEK:

Looking at the Trail Behind

Celebrate Your Wins & Learn From Your Loses

Mind

What was my goal?

What went well?

What didnt go so well?
And how can I learn from it?

Soul

What was my goal?

What went well?

What didnt go so well?
And how can I learn from it?

additional thoughts:

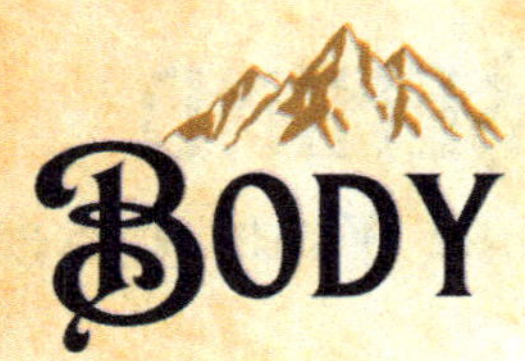

Body

What was my goal?

What went well?

What didn't go so well?
And how can I learn from it?

Relationships

What was my goal?

What went well?

What didn't go so well?
And how can I learn from it?

additional thoughts:

Check out this week's
Inspiring recording!
date:
THE 90-DAY
MSBR Journal
WEEK
10

EXPLORE
reflect & WRITE

EXPLORE
reflect & WRITE

EXPLORE
reflect & WRITE

EXPLORE
reflect & WRITE

Paths to progress

This Week's MSBR Goals

MIND...

SOUL...

BODY..

RELATIONSHIPS....

general stuff

I HAVE TO DO THIS WEEK

- [ ]
- [ ]
- [ ]
- [ ]
- [ ]
- [ ]
- [ ]
- [ ]
- [ ]
- [ ]
- [ ]
- [ ]
- [ ]
- [ ]
- [ ]
- [ ]
- [ ]
- [ ]
- [ ]
- [ ]
- [ ]
- [ ]
- [ ]
- [ ]
- [ ]

SUNDAY

TIME GOAL / TASK M/S/B/R

- ☐
- ☐
- ☐
- ☐
- ☐
- ☐

TIME GOAL / TASK M/S/B/R

- ☐
- ☐
- ☐
- ☐
- ☐
- ☐

MONDAY

TIME GOAL / TASK M/S/B/R

- ☐
- ☐
- ☐
- ☐
- ☐
- ☐

TIME GOAL / TASK M/S/B/R

- ☐
- ☐
- ☐
- ☐
- ☐
- ☐

TUESDAY

TIME GOAL / TASK M/S/B/R

- ☐
- ☐
- ☐
- ☐
- ☐
- ☐

TIME GOAL / TASK M/S/B/R

- ☐
- ☐
- ☐
- ☐
- ☐
- ☐

WEDNESDAY

TIME GOAL / TASK M/S/B/R

- ☐
- ☐
- ☐
- ☐
- ☐
- ☐

TIME GOAL / TASK M/S/B/R

- ☐
- ☐
- ☐
- ☐
- ☐
- ☐

THURSDAY

TIME	GOAL / TASK	M/S/B/R
☐		
☐		
☐		
☐		
☐		
☐		

TIME	GOAL / TASK	M/S/B/R
☐		
☐		
☐		
☐		
☐		
☐		

FRIDAY

TIME	GOAL / TASK	M/S/B/R
☐		
☐		
☐		
☐		
☐		
☐		

TIME	GOAL / TASK	M/S/B/R
☐		
☐		
☐		
☐		
☐		
☐		

SATURDAY

TIME	GOAL / TASK	M/S/B/R
☐		
☐		
☐		
☐		
☐		
☐		

TIME	GOAL / TASK	M/S/B/R
☐		
☐		
☐		
☐		
☐		
☐		

MY INSIGHT OF THE WEEK:

Looking at the Trail Behind

Celebrate Your Wins & Learn From Your Loses

Mind

What was my goal?

What went well?

What didn't go so well?
And how can I learn from it?

Soul

What was my goal?

What went well?

What didn't go so well?
And how can I learn from it?

additional thoughts:

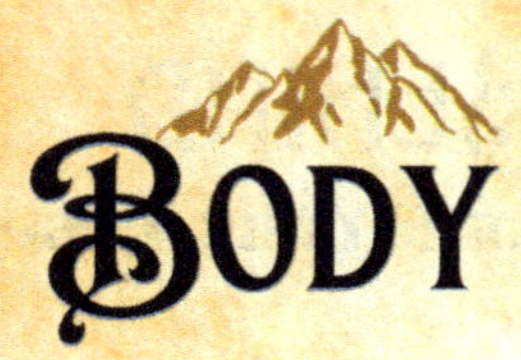

Body

What was my goal?

What went well?

What didnt go so well?
And how can I learn from it?

Relationships

What was my goal?

What went well?

What didnt go so well?
And how can I learn from it?

additional thoughts:

Check out this week's
Inspiring recording!
date:
THE 90-DAY
MSBR Journal
WEEK
11

EXPLORE
reflect & WRITE

EXPLORE
reflect & WRITE

EXPLORE
reflect & WRITE

EXPLORE
reflect & WRITE

Paths to progress

This Weeks MSBR Goals

MIND...

SOUL...

BODY..

RELATIONSHIPS....

general stuff

I HAVE TO DO THIS WEEK

SUNDAY

TIME	GOAL / TASK	M/S/B/R	TIME	GOAL / TASK	M/S/B/R
☐			☐		
☐			☐		
☐			☐		
☐			☐		
☐			☐		
☐			☐		

MONDAY

TIME	GOAL / TASK	M/S/B/R	TIME	GOAL / TASK	M/S/B/R
☐			☐		
☐			☐		
☐			☐		
☐			☐		
☐			☐		
☐			☐		

TUESDAY

TIME	GOAL / TASK	M/S/B/R	TIME	GOAL / TASK	M/S/B/R
☐			☐		
☐			☐		
☐			☐		
☐			☐		
☐			☐		
☐			☐		

WEDNESDAY

TIME	GOAL / TASK	M/S/B/R	TIME	GOAL / TASK	M/S/B/R
☐			☐		
☐			☐		
☐			☐		
☐			☐		
☐			☐		
☐			☐		

THURSDAY

TIME	GOAL / TASK	M/S/B/R
☐		
☐		
☐		
☐		
☐		
☐		

TIME	GOAL / TASK	M/S/B/R
☐		
☐		
☐		
☐		
☐		
☐		

FRIDAY

TIME	GOAL / TASK	M/S/B/R
☐		
☐		
☐		
☐		
☐		
☐		

TIME	GOAL / TASK	M/S/B/R
☐		
☐		
☐		
☐		
☐		
☐		

SATURDAY

TIME	GOAL / TASK	M/S/B/R
☐		
☐		
☐		
☐		
☐		
☐		

TIME	GOAL / TASK	M/S/B/R
☐		
☐		
☐		
☐		
☐		
☐		

MY INSIGHT OF THE WEEK:

Looking at the Trail Behind

Celebrate Your Wins & Learn From Your Loses

Mind

What was my goal?

What went well?

What didn't go so well?
And how can I learn from it?

Soul

What was my goal?

What went well?

What didn't go so well?
And how can I learn from it?

additional thoughts:

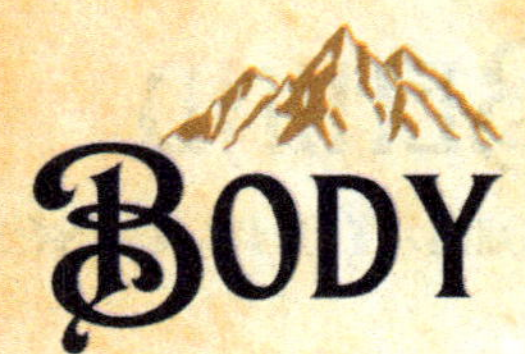

BODY

What was my goal?

What went well?

What didnt go so well?
And how can I learn from it?

RELATIONSHIPS

What was my goal?

What went well?

What didnt go so well?
And how can I learn from it?

additional thoughts:

Check out this week's
Inspiring recording!
date:
THE 90-DAY
MSBR Journal
WEEK
12

WEEK **12** THE 90-DAY
MSBR Journal

As the final curtain falls on our 12-week journaling adventure, take a bow for the goals you've set and the strides you've made. This isn't the end; it's a standing ovation to your dedicated growth and formidable resilience. Carry the lessons, savor the wins, and let this closing scene be a prelude to exciting new acts. Write on with confidence, and may the next chapters be as captivating as the journey you've penned in these transformative weeks. Until we meet again in Volume Two, cheers to you, the author of your remarkable story!

Here are some suggested topics to journal about this week:

1 MINDSET SHIFTS

- Reflecting on the journal from Week 1 to the present, what particular changes in your mindset have become apparent over the course of the last 12 weeks?

2 CHALLENGES & GROWTH

- How did you approach challenges differently over the last 12 weeks compared to the beginning of the journal?
- In what ways have you grown mentally and emotionally during these 12 weeks?

3 POSITIVE ACTIONS/ HABITS

- What positive habits or rituals have you cultivated over the past 12 weeks that contributed to your mindset development?
- Have you established new routines in the last 12 weeks that align with your desired mindset?

4 HANDLING SETBACKS

- Reflecting on the last 12 weeks, how did you handle setbacks or failures, and has your approach evolved?
- What lessons did you learn from setbacks during these 12 weeks that influenced your mindset?

5 MINDFULNESS & AWARENESS

- Did you become more mindful of your thoughts and attitudes over the last 12 weeks?
- How has increased self-awareness in the last 12 weeks influenced your mindset?

6 RELATIONSHIPS & COMMUNICATION

- How did your mindset over the last 12 weeks influence your interactions with others?
- Did you notice any improvements in your communication/boundaries style during these 12 weeks?

EXPLORE
reflect & WRITE

EXPLORE
reflect & WRITE

EXPLORE
reflect &
WRITE

EXPLORE
reflect & WRITE

Paths to progress

This Week's MSBR Goals

MIND...

SOUL...

BODY..

RELATIONSHIPS....

general stuff

I HAVE TO DO THIS WEEK

SUNDAY

TIME	GOAL / TASK	M/S/B/R
	☐	
	☐	
	☐	
	☐	
	☐	
	☐	

TIME	GOAL / TASK	M/S/B/R
	☐	
	☐	
	☐	
	☐	
	☐	
	☐	

MONDAY

TIME	GOAL / TASK	M/S/B/R
	☐	
	☐	
	☐	
	☐	
	☐	
	☐	

TIME	GOAL / TASK	M/S/B/R
	☐	
	☐	
	☐	
	☐	
	☐	
	☐	

TUESDAY

TIME	GOAL / TASK	M/S/B/R
	☐	
	☐	
	☐	
	☐	
	☐	
	☐	

TIME	GOAL / TASK	M/S/B/R
	☐	
	☐	
	☐	
	☐	
	☐	
	☐	

WEDNESDAY

TIME	GOAL / TASK	M/S/B/R
	☐	
	☐	
	☐	
	☐	
	☐	
	☐	

TIME	GOAL / TASK	M/S/B/R
	☐	
	☐	
	☐	
	☐	
	☐	
	☐	

THURSDAY

TIME	GOAL / TASK	M/S/B/R
☐		
☐		
☐		
☐		
☐		
☐		

TIME	GOAL / TASK	M/S/B/R
☐		
☐		
☐		
☐		
☐		
☐		

FRIDAY

TIME	GOAL / TASK	M/S/B/R
☐		
☐		
☐		
☐		
☐		
☐		

TIME	GOAL / TASK	M/S/B/R
☐		
☐		
☐		
☐		
☐		
☐		

SATURDAY

TIME	GOAL / TASK	M/S/B/R
☐		
☐		
☐		
☐		
☐		
☐		

TIME	GOAL / TASK	M/S/B/R
☐		
☐		
☐		
☐		
☐		
☐		

MY INSIGHT OF THE WEEK:

Looking at the Trail Behind

Celebrate Your Wins & Learn From Your Loses

Mind

What was my goal?

What went well?

What didnt go so well?
And how can I learn from it?

Soul

What was my goal?

What went well?

What didnt go so well?
And how can I learn from it?

additional thoughts:

Body

What was my goal?

What went well?

What didnt go so well?
And how can I learn from it?

Relationships

What was my goal?

What went well?

What didnt go so well?
And how can I learn from it?

additional thoughts:

notes

notes

notes

notes

ENDNOTES

1 AKIBA BEN JOSEPH - JewishEncyclopedia.com. (n.d.). https://www.jewishencyclopedia.com/articles/1033-akiba-ben-joseph

2 Rusk, R. D., & Waters, L. (2015). A psycho-social system approach to well-being: Empirically deriving the Five Domains of Positive Functioning. The Journal of Positive Psychology, 10(2), 141–152. https://doi.org/10.1080/17439760.2014.920409

3 In the mystical Jewish teachings. Endnote- Kabbalistic teachings of Etz Haim (Yitzchak Luria 1534-1572)

4 Stoker, B. (1993). Dracula. Wordsworth Editions. Originally published in 1987

5 Mcleod, S. (2023, November 24). Maslow's Hierarchy of Needs. Simply Psychology. https://www.simplypsychology.org/maslow.html

WHY YOU WONT FIND US ON SOCIAL MEDIA?

In a world dominated by algorithms and corporate influence, we've opted for an alternative approach. You won't spot us amid the facade of manufactured 'likes' or the illusion of 'friends' shaped by code and social media. We champion authenticity. You're here because someone genuine, who grasps our ethos, believed in our connection. Perhaps a trusted friend or someone who genuinely values you recommended us. Maybe our book caught your eye in a store, or perhaps the universe orchestrated our meeting for this journey together. Let's step forward together on a path where the most significant algorithms are those etched within your heart.

about THE AUTHOR

Chaim Levy is a multifaceted individual with a diverse portfolio spanning education, non-profit, and real estate, initiatives. His life is a testament to a profound commitment to making a positive impact on the world. As the founder and head of the non-profit organization Gosephardic, Chaim has spearheaded various projects, including the establishment of Camp Gesher—a nurturing haven for children from broken homes and orphans, where volunteers unite to create a supportive environment.

In the realm of education, Chaim serves as the Educational Director of a girls' seminary in Jerusalem, playing a pivotal role in the intellectual and personal development of students. His influence extends to educational institutions in New York, Los Angeles, and Montreal, where his unique perspective and unwavering dedication have left an indelible mark on each community.

This book, a culmination of Chaim's experiences and insights, embodies the essence of balance and a holistic view. Through his worldwide programs, he has not only facilitated the creation of hundreds of marriages for students but has also woven a narrative that reflects a life dedicated to service, education, and the harmonious celebration of enduring connections. Readers can expect a captivating journey that inspires them to embrace empathy, resilience, and the transformative power of community—a true reflection of Chaim Levy's commitment to creating balance in every aspect of life.

Register to be paired with an accountability partner!

EMAIL us at:

Visit our website:

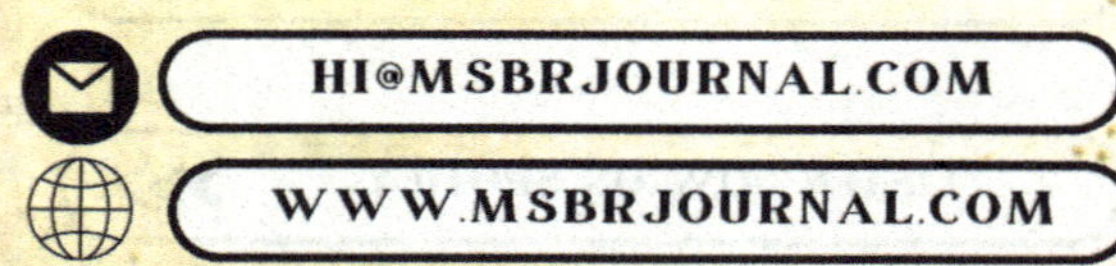

Watch for the Release of

MSBR JOURNAL VOLUME TWO

Made in the USA
Columbia, SC
04 February 2025

52401815R00102